This book is dedicated to my teacher, Mrs. Johnson.

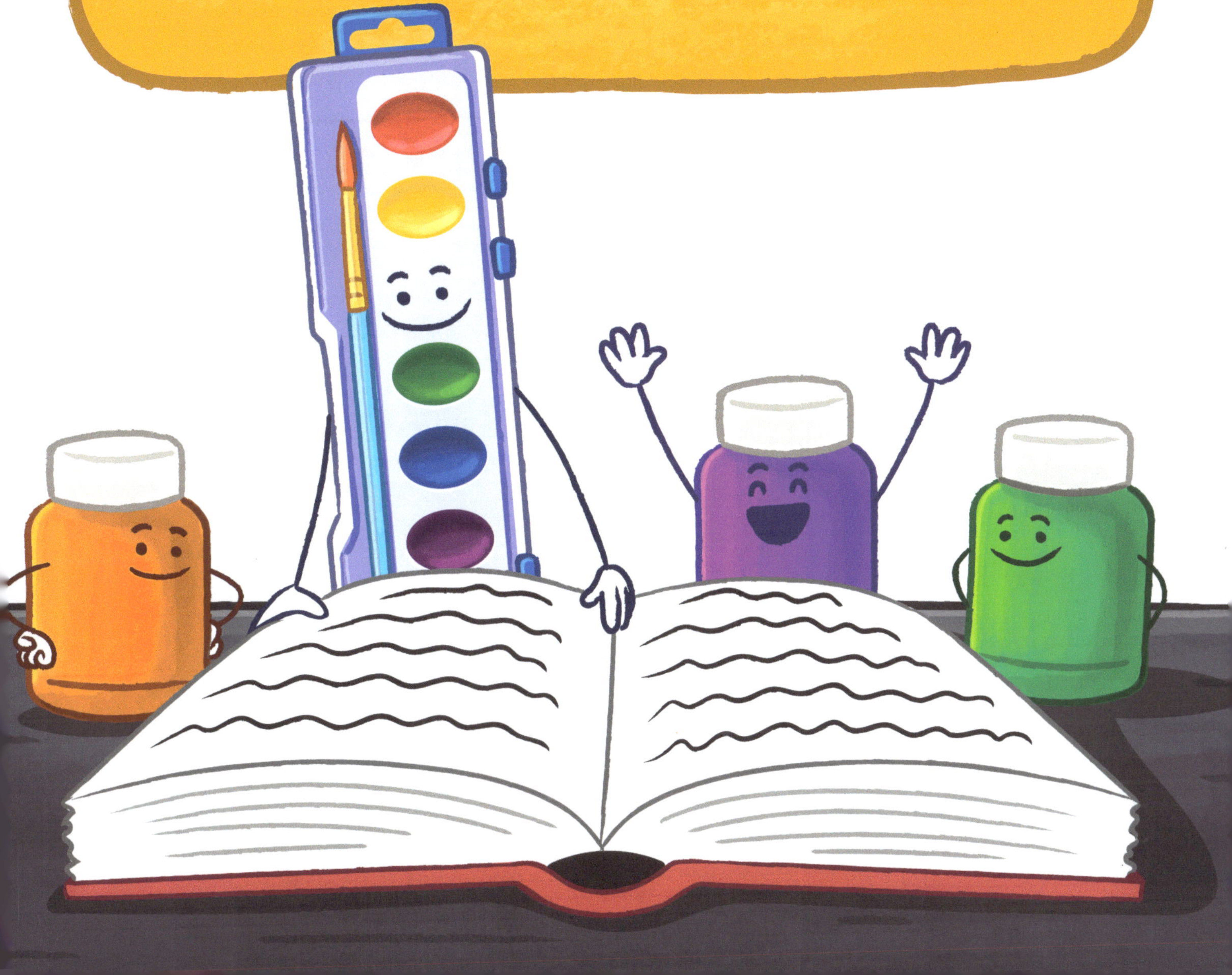

Copyright © 2023 Jennifer Jones
All copyright laws and rights reserved. Published in the U.S.A.
For more information, email info@ninjalifehacks.tv
Paperback ISBN: 978-1-63731-855-3 Hardcover ISBN: 978-1-63731-857-7
eBook ISBN: 978-1-63731-856-0

Find the Paints on Strike lesson plans at ninjalifehacks.tv

Imagine what it's like
to bring color to the world,
to brighten up art projects
for every boy and girl.

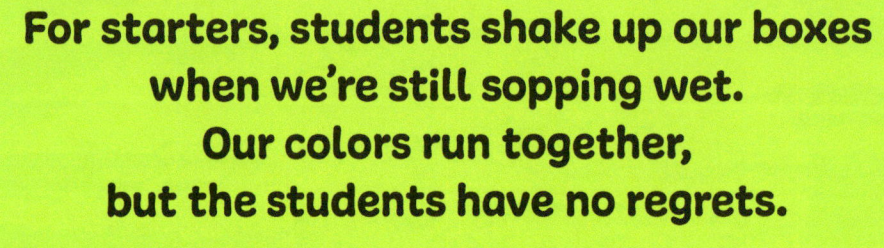

For starters, students shake up our boxes
when we're still sopping wet.
Our colors run together,
but the students have no regrets.

The paints that are in pots
don't have it much better at all.
Students dump us out on the floor,
and it's horrible when the kids slip and fall!

The students never seem to get it
or even seem to try
to use only a *little* bit of paint on the paper,
so that their project has time to dry.

Until they learn to treat us right
and be careful with us paints,
we are going on STRIKE.
And we will tell them our complaints!

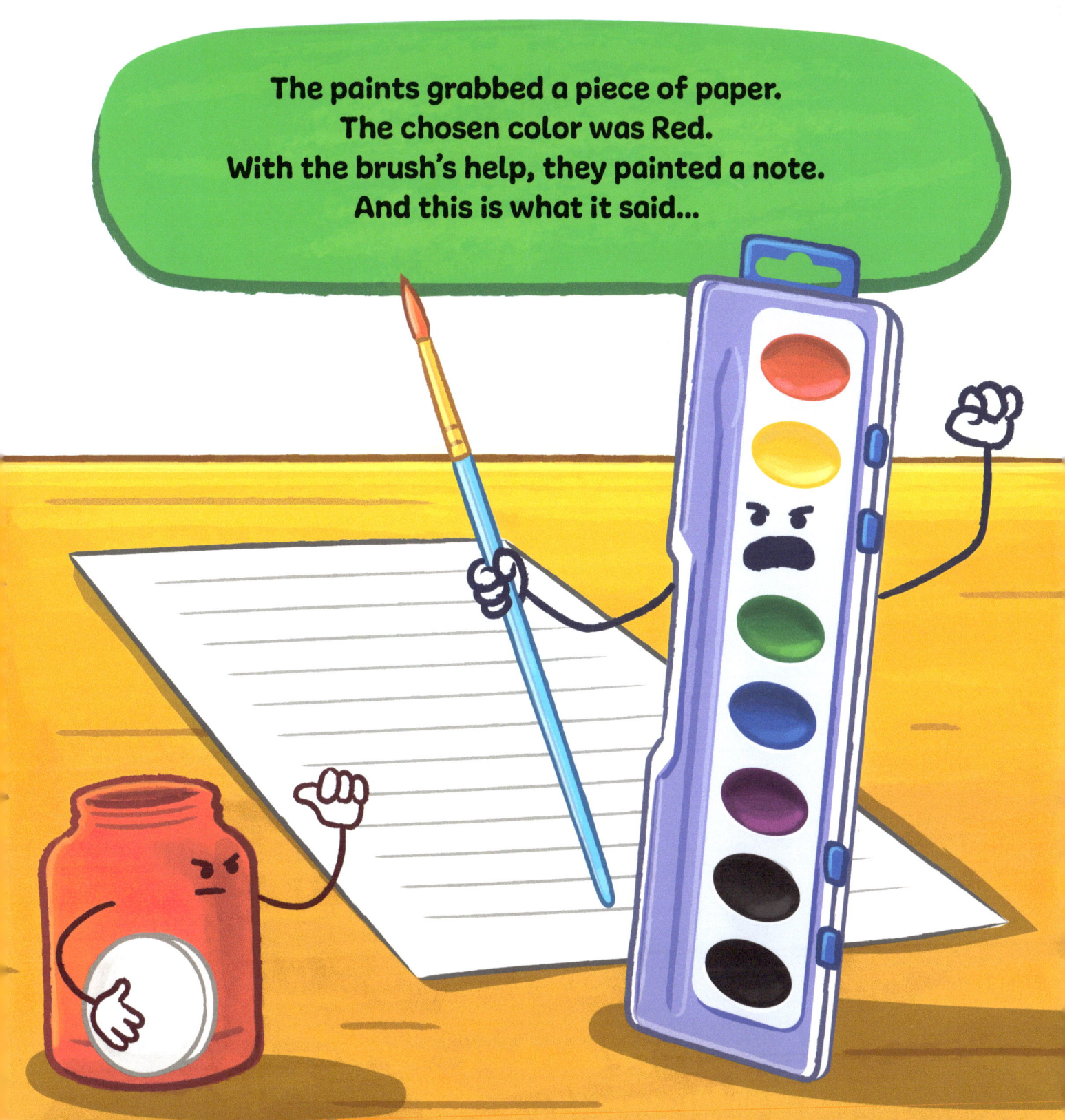

You mess with us and dry us out,

leaving brushes in our pots.

You say that we are important to your

schoolwork,

but clearly we are not!

Until you treat us properly,

and not however you would like,

consider us paints out of commission.

THE PAINTS ARE GOING ON STRIKE!

www.ingramcontent.com/pod-product-compliance
Lightning Source LLC
Chambersburg PA
CBHW041525070526
44585CB00002B/81